Life After Life

Robin K. Dhillon.

Order this book online at www.trafford.com
or email orders@trafford.com

Most Trafford titles are also available at major online book retailers.

© Copyright 2009 Robin K. Dhillon.

All rights reserved. No part of this publication may be reproduced, stored in a retrieval system, or transmitted, in any form or by any means, electronic, mechanical, photocopying, recording, or otherwise, without the written prior permission of the author.

Photography by: Philip Dhillon

Printed in Victoria, BC, Canada.

ISBN: 978-1-4251-7262-6 (Soft)

Our mission is to efficiently provide the world's finest, most comprehensive book publishing service, enabling every author to experience success. To find out how to publish your book, your way, and have it available worldwide, visit us online at www.trafford.com/

Trafford rev: 11/09/09

www.trafford.com

North America & international
toll-free: 1 888 232 4444 (USA & Canada)
phone: 250 383 6864 ♦ fax: 812 355 4082

TABLE OF CONTENTS

Dedication	5
Acknowledgements	7
Summary	9
A Walking Talking Story	11
Singapore	16
Malaysia	19
Moss Co.	25
Spokaloo	27
Cold Facts	29
The Guad Squad	34
Americans at UAG	36
The City of Love	39
Love in the City	42
Dixie	45
Have Knife, Will Travel	51
Nugent Came Back	53
Michael, John, Wayne, and Me	54
Before The End of These Days	56

Dedication

I would like to dedicate this book to my friend, wife, and soul mate. She knows why because in my irritating and perseverating fashion I tell her every day. As has been said, "Life is short. Be swift to love! Make haste to be kind!" -Henri Frederic Amiel philosopher and writer (1821-1881)

Robin K. Dhillon, M.D., M.B.A.

Acknowledgements

Many thanks to the following who believed my antics and silliness recorded and published might just be worth the laughs generated. So much so that many of them contributed their hard-earned money which allowed for publication of this book:

Dave Batsdorf (Dave, in his quiet way is very loud. Thank you, Dave.)

Jenny Bonarrigo (If not for Jenny, I would still be lost. But, now, I'm found.)

Reno Bucca (who in a different time and in a different persona danced and taught others to do the same and today in a different time and a different place has taught many of us and brought us closer to God)

Peter Daniel & Ana Rosa Buckman, M. D., F.A.C.S. (Two friends in all times. Gracias a ustedes, por tanto.)

Tom Campanella (Leading us all into a new future in Healthcare)

Chuck & Christine (Carbone-)Maurer—Anthony's folks (another "lost" son, like Kyle and, yet, not like Kyle, more like Ant.)

Anthony Maurer (who brings out the best in A.D. and makes us both laugh)

Dan & Patti Cathcart (If anybody in St. Francis Xavier parish, Medina, Ohio doesn't know Dan and his good works, they are either very new or very oblivious)

Melissa Clendenin (Wild AND Innocent…an unbeatable combination! God love her, I know we all do. Forgive me for being truthful; I can only do it with true friends-Michael keeps her in line.)

Leafie Dempsey (Leafie's Daddy is Sicilian, from the old country, and she grows tomatoes in her garden … can I say more?)

Sharon M. Dhillon (who makes life livable for us all)

Kathryn M. Dhillon (the only one I know who could make life more fun and interesting than it already is)

Aleksander K. Dhillon (one who has taught me about inborn and native talent and kindness in everything from baseball to mathematics and life in general)

Nikolai B. Dhillon (my last best hope to know a bit more about life outside of my ken and one that always comes through with the goods)

Ron & Deanna Eastwood (two very different people who warm our—all of our—hearts)

Karam Singh & Gurbachan Kaur Dhillon, MD-my parents who I knew and yet didn't know. I owe to them all that I am (as my Papa always said about his mother). I lived with them both, when they were together and when they were alone. It is funny how things come back to me of what they said as I grow older and how much better I know them now compared to what I knew then.

James & Audrey Dhillon & their four boys-Jesse, Daniel, Philip, & Kley-who have all played their part and taught me a li'l sum'pin 'bout a li'l sum'pin-Aud, when we talk I remember Bruno, Sachi, & Bobby, when life was never going to change or end. Lyamya.

Barb Freeman (With intelligence and education, Barb has maintained an even keel and a sense of humor.)

Dave & Donna Haney (with each additional child the entire world seems to wonder why? I, on the other hand, am amazed at their ability to continue their forward progress while supporting so many. I would congratulate Dave, however, he has already done that himself, and Donna is the one truly able to put it all together.)

Bobby J. Heath, MD (who not only taught me but showed me how to care, not just for people with sick hearts, but for people)

Reverend Mark L. Hollis (who lived up to his promise and brought me closer to God)

Mike & Lynn Hulthen (two people whom I cannot say enough about—all good, Mike)

Kyle Hulthen (one who has my heart and like me is always ready, to "Rock The Casbah!")

Barb & the Four Little Imbrugias (the 4 would be 0 without the 1)

Susan Kuznik (turning the ordinary into extraordinary)

Rick Luzader & Anne Kennedy (a pair that I could spend years listening to and learning from ... I don't think they know that; I've been too bashful to say it to them openly)

Dave & Marci Martinez (A.K.A. The Rodriguezes ... nota bene: this is from Dr. Evil.)

Mike & Becky Mohoney (who have baseball in their blood and kindness in their hearts)

Holly Monchein (A fellow traveler)

Patrick H. & Jeanne Norris (Both of whom know how to give even when they ain't got)

Jackie Punka (my favorite P. A.)

Joel & Beth Riegelmayer (who live with smiles that hit us all)

Kurt & Bonnie Schwemm (how they both put up with 'the dog,' I don't know, but, Kurt, we all still love you)

Param Srikantia (an experience to be lived)

Annette & Oron Wilcox (living lives of giving)

E. Taliaferro Warren, MD (who taught me many things, not the least of which was how to be truly gentle in Surgery and in life and encouraged an appreciation of the finer things in life, especially cooking, music, fine dining, and fine wines…oh, there's so much more…thank you, T. W.)

Marshall Watson (who, I have only come to realize now, made me look good and truly saved lives—patients and residents—even when I was a bumbling fool barely able to pronounce "Cardiothoracic Surgeon," let alone do the job!)

Corrie Zimerla (who with intelligence and humor is as good a friend as she is a mom)

A note of caution: I have changed the names to protect the innocent (whom I am certain are associated with the folks mentioned in the book). If you are looking for your own character be wary, you might not be there (I may be saving you for another story…).

Robin K. Dhillon, M.D., M.B.A.

Summary

This is a story about a young man who began life in South East Asia, grew up there and in the Pacific Northwest, became a physician and surgeon, later developed Multiple Sclerosis and had to give up his vocation and avocation—surgery—and found the true essence of his life—his wife and children. Along with his wife and children was a love of humanity and the world around that originally led him into pursuing Medicine as a career. Once again this is a story that proves how true it is that, as Yogi Berra once said, "it ain't over, till it's over." IT AIN'T OVER!

Robin K. Dhillon, M.D., M.B.A.

A Walking Talking Story

In beginning the telling of this tale, I wondered what should go into this story. Is it worth telling? To whom would I tell this story? Should it be written or simply passed on to family and friends in oral fashion? This is my story from birth to today and looking at it and thinking about it I find that it is an interesting story, rich in background and the many twists and turns of life. In many ways it is much like the billions of stories that make up the lives on this planet. Yet it has many messages for all those who read, enjoy a good tale, love the intricacies of life, and can appreciate the hard-earned lessons contained herein. I believe the audience for this story consists of all who like to read and either enjoy or would like to enjoy life. Enjoying life in my thoughts does not consist of hedonistic partying without end. No, enjoying life consists of following one of coach Alex's worthy rules (coach Alex is a baseball player and coaches children at a college summer baseball camp), which is a question and answer as follows. "Why do we do what is right?" He asks the children in camp this question. His answer is, "Because it makes us better." How simple. And, yet, how true. Thank you, coach Alex. As in baseball, so in life. Like so many stories that find meaning in children's games and in life and manage to do it in both at the same time I believe it is worth telling. Others can see the parallels in their lives and make good use of the many hidden smiles that will light their way forward into a life that is right...to a life that is better.

This story began with me having a great deal of time on my hands. I lived through the great depression. Not after the stock market crash in 1929, but rather seventy years later after my own personal crash in 1999. My personal crash had nothing to do with rapid declines of stock values on Wall Street and analysts plummeting headfirst to the pavement below. No, when I had my crash, stocks were soaring to unheard of heights everyone with a dollar in their pocket at the beginning of the year seemed to be very proud of how that dollar had, by some financial version of mitosis, grown to become more than just one dollar. I, typical of the classic version of most physicians, have never had any understanding of money and finances. It has often been said of me—by me as often as anyone—that if I had a dollar in my pocket, I would find a way to give away two! For any who might begin to read this story in the hopes of learning how to acquire the riches I have acquired in life, although it can be done if one keeps one's eyes and mind open, I will caution you here in the beginning. The riches that I have look back at me with loving eyes. They do not always laugh at my jokes—occasionally I will happen upon one that is actually funny—and I will not always laugh at theirs but we always try. There is no scheme within that will succeed to produce financial riches for the reader. As Harry Truman once wrote, "I always did let ethics beat me out of money and I suppose I always will." (The Wit and Wisdom of Harry S. Truman, ed. Alex Ayres, A Meridian Book, ISBN 0-452-01182-5, 1998) This is not a guide but rather a description of how one boy saw the world smiling, smiled back, grew to be a man, forgot how to smile for a while, then through a strange twist of fate, which some might consider unfortunate, saw the world smiling again and learned again how to return that smile. This is a story of a young man who conquers the world and then sets it free so that all can live happily. In doing so, I find that, only now, have I truly conquered the world and countless galaxies beyond this one.

It seems strange how, at times, one's earlier life seems to echo one's later life. When I was a boy I grew up in a tropical climate and, like many who grew up there, did not much care for shoes. Everywhere I went, I went barefoot. Whenever my father bought me shoes, I managed, without thinking or trying, to lose them. I really did not like wearing shoes. The roads there were made of dirt—with heavy deposits of red clay and iron pyrite—and gravel. My feet became very tough and endured what people used to shoes would find to be very uncomfortable and, even, painful. Today I find that with Multiple Sclerosis my feet are extremely uncomfortable in shoes and I am much more comfortable when barefoot. Yet, the only predictability is life's lack of predictability. It does not fit into a neat little package since at the same time I cannot stand the heat. Whereas in my youth I lived outside in a tropical climate with ambient temperatures in the low one hundreds, today a temperature in the eighties will have me prostrate and begging for water and air-conditioning.

This story could have had many titles but I chose one of my favorites which probably only has meaning for me. One that carries a great deal of truth and explains, in many ways, how I evolved from who I was to who I am, would have been, "Forty, Going On Four." This was a favorite and, in many ways, has been difficult to relinquish. I missed being home with my oldest two children and did not witness them making the transition from crawling to walking. With my youngest, who turned four while I was in my early forties and while I made some of the greatest discoveries of my life, I had the good fortune to witness this magical moment in his life. With that momentous occasion and the ensuing discoveries I have had the good fortune to make I have learned many things from him about life and living. He has been one of my most enduring, profound, and prolific teachers on how to live life and what is important in living it.

Within this moment going from crawling to walking is a truly magical experience. I wonder how many fathers have never witnessed it and how many times mothers have, without realizing that father missed it. I wonder especially because I almost missed it. By some stroke of great luck I happened to witness it and am still re-creating it in my mind's eye and reliving it. Houdini may have created the image and the atmosphere of magic but this truly was magic. It continues to exude magic as I continue to be captivated by the lessons that the young ones in the family have to impart even though they may not realize they are not only going to school but also teaching school. They live a life where they are loved and reading and games are fun and fun is their task in life. They are educating me without trying and within that picture is a concept worthy of the greatest teacher and philosopher. From all of this I have learned to watch the littlest ones among us, at home, in church, at the movies, everywhere, and from them I learn how to have fun.

I walk and I talk. Still. And I worry about being able to do that each and every day because it is no longer easy and natural. Like any story it does not begin here but sometimes it makes more sense to take stock of your current situation, then look back to where and how it began, and to appreciate today with the 'retrospec-toscope' (this is a fictional 'scope that is referred to by surgery attending physicians, especially at surgical morbidity and mortality meetings, to encourage young surgical residents to look back on the how and why of things that happen to their patients, especially because of the residents' actions or lack of action, so that they may avoid the same problems in the future and have better results for their patients in the future) in full view. As I look back and take a walk through my own life, I find that there is much to talk about. It is truly amazing that there are so many human lives out there; each with a story to tell. With these thoughts and some time, after twenty years of living '24-7' and hoping for a few extra seconds each day to do what needed to be done I set out to tell my story which in some respects seems fanciful but turns out to be truer than true and allows for several insights into life, love, and the pursuit of happiness.

I find that as I walk and I talk about this story that is my life I have made some monumental discoveries at a relatively young age that many men and women do not discover until their dotage. In your dotage, you dote. Dote is a word that comes from a Middle English word 'doten,' which, in turn, is derived from a Middle Dutch word 'doten,' which means be silly. It fits and yet it does not seem quite complimentary. Somehow there is greatness in the silliness that old people and children enjoy. I have found that somewhere in these great and silly acts and activities exists the wonder and beauty of life. So, some day, I hope to dote.

Among my discoveries I find that despite thinking that my big discovery has been that I walk and I talk, the truth is that I ran through life in a fast forward fashion for many years as quickly as I could. At the same time I did not speak and in many ways when I kept my mouth shut I was much better off and, even though they did not realize it, most people who knew me were very thankful. It seemed I did not have time to wait for anything or anyone. Patience was not one of my strong suits.

In fact, it hardly seemed possible for me. In living life that way I was very well suited to surgery, especially cardiac surgery. Yet I also pushed myself very hard and drove myself to the end of the road very quickly. The end of that road was to lead to another road which is leading forward into the unknown at present but the view from here is quite captivating, has a bright, clear, blue sky above and my wife and children in full view. I have to say that if I could sing without every cat in the neighborhood immediately begging for me to stop I would.

They say you are what you eat. In a sense that is true but not necessarily in obvious ways. It may be simply that the food you eat growing up is a reflection of where you grow up. Ultimately you are whom you are, to paraphrase Popeye, because of where you grow up and who walks (or eats) ahead, behind, and beside you. I grew up, as I will describe in the chapters to come, in a large number of places across the world. The beginnings of life for me were in Malaysia where a rather unique blend of cultures formed a curious and unique environment of foods, sights, and people after World War Two. One of those people is myself. Among the many cultures who have flourished here are Malays, Chinese, Indians, Dutch, British, Japanese, Americans, and many others. As described in a special report from the Washington Times on Malaysia on April 28, 1999, "Even though there is [sic] a strong linguistic and cultural ties, especially among the Chinese and Indian communities, the spirit of Malaysian nationhood transcends ethnicity. In this respect, they are similar to American ethnic groups who consider themselves Americans with an ethnic qualifier."

The food in Malaysia reflects the many influences of many cultures and many people. In Singapore the Nonya culture that is as unique as a culture can be since it only exists in that island nation and nowhere else has an equally unique cuisine. From satay and Tiger beer to spaghetti bolognese at the Selangor Club, I find my own identity embroiled. It seems strange yet I can describe certain things like plain white rice with ketchup to people who grew up among the Malays despite not being Malay and we all have an instant understanding of how right and good life is. I do not know why but the foods I grew up with seem to define a different sensibility about life. A very Malay sensibility. It is very hot in Malaysia and I believe that the saying that only mad dogs and Englishmen venture out in the noonday sun originated here. My father has often told of his amazement with the Malays—Sikhs, like my father, grew up different from Malays, like me—with a story. When he was first in Malaysia he remembered seeing a Malaysian man who was supposed to be working on the roads. In the course of the day when the sun was at its zenith and bearing down at its hottest this road worker took off his shirt, with a stick fashioned a canopy, and took a long nap. For the Englishmen and my father, the hours during the day are very important for all the work one can accomplish. For the Malay, and for me, the hours during the day are as important as the hours during the night and not more important. For me I believe that at night it is good to sleep. If one can recreate that heaven on earth—sleep—during the day then one has powers that are beyond those of most mere humans. Much like young children, whose powers extend far beyond those of mere humans, those who can sleep within moments of their heads hitting their pillows, or lying under the shade of a shirt in the tropical sun, are those who sleep the sleep of the righteous. After twenty years of sleep-deprivation I have had to learn to reacquire this state of mind and being. This is the journey I am taking with this story.

It has been a long journey and each day seems to blend into the last. Some of that is related to my memory deficit. It seems that now I can remember events for at least eleven hours. However, forget eleven hours and one minute. Literally, I forget about it! I guess that is part of what they call a cognitive deficit. Of course, I remembered that. A cognitive deficit is good and bad. Good since I do not have to remember everything and have a physical reason for not doing so. Bad because I forget too many things. Sometimes I even forget stuff I want to remember, like why I just walked downstairs when I have stuff to do upstairs. So much of life seems to be that way. Good and bad. Up and down. It pays to forget the downs and enjoy the ups for as long as they last.

Among the good things I remember are a great many people. My favorites all bring a smile to my face not only when I visit with them but also when I think of them. I think life is a story that can be connected to all those people that one meets during life and one gets to know along the way. Much like a journey, which is marked by the interesting sites on the trip, only these sites are interactive. In a way it has been a preview of the wonderful and fancy things (or as they say in farm country—trick and fancy) that the computer age has wrought. I have heard that in the richest man in the world's home a computer, which senses each human's moods and feelings, adjusts the environment accordingly. Human beings have been doing this for eons. They hear your voice, see your face, smell your scent, feel your presence, and taste your mood. As they do they modify your environment. Unlike computers you can return the favor and modify their environment as well.

I think back to my earliest days. Although I do not consciously remember being born, I know I was born in Singapore. I have been there afterwards and remember it in the nineteen-sixties just as I remember Malaysia where I grew up until 1969.

Singapore

The story starts in the island nation of Singapore, 137 kilometers (85 miles) north of the Equator[1].

In 1819 Sir Stamford Raffles founded a British settlement at the island of Singapore[2]. *Sir Thomas Stamford Raffles* was the British East Indian administrator and founder of the port city of Singapore who was largely responsible for the creation of Britain's Far Eastern empire. He was knighted in 1816[3]. Interestingly, at least for me with my love of the great diversity of people the world over, he was a strong advocate of the Malays and was well liked not only in Penang but London as well.

Singapore in 2006.

---

1   http://en.wikipedia.org/wiki/Singapore
2   http://www.lukemastin.com/history/georgian_britain.html

3   **"Raffles, Sir Stamford."** Encyclopædia Britannica. 2006. Encyclopædia Britannica Premium Service. 1 Aug. 2006 <http://www.britannica.com/eb/article-9062451>.

Robin K. Dhillon, M.D., M.B.A.

The Singaporean flag

Singapore was a Malay fishing village when it was colonized by the United Kingdom in the 19th century. During World War II was occupied by Japan, and then became part of the merger, which established the Federation of Malaysia.[4]

In researching the origins of Singapore its historical origins become lost in the echoes of time. Although some of the echoes reflect from China, some from India, some from Indonesia, some from Holland, some from England, there are so many echoes that the resulting sound has many flavors and a uniquely Singaporean resonance.

Singapore in 1958 was still a colony of the United Kingdom and part of the Federation of Malaya. Malays, Chinese, Indians, and a smattering of Europeans populated it. In seafaring days it was known as the crossroads of the world. In many ways it still is the crossroads of the world even in the era of air travel. When I was born there were only a few major hospitals in the region. My older sister had been born by caesarian section at the hospital (The **Kandang Kerbau Women's and Children's Hospital** (abbrev: **KKH**; It is the largest hospital specializing in healthcare for women and children in Singapore. From a 30-bed maternity hospital founded in 1924, it has grown into an 888-bed hospital providing obstetric and gynecology, neonatology and pediatric services. Often affectionately referred to as "KK" amongst locals, it is the birthplace of a sizeable proportion of Singaporeans, delivering over half of total newborns in the country as early as 1938.[5]) in Singapore four years previously. I could not wait and demonstrated a character trait, which has been a personal trademark ever since—impatience. Before my father and sister arrived from Malaysia and before the obstetrician could get ready to do a repeat caesarian section on my mother I came out screaming via the birth canal precluding any other route of birth. After countless years of school from first grade to medical school even though I was what is commonly called a "V-back" delivery, i.e., a vaginal delivery after a woman has had a previous Caesarian section I had never actually seen one! No, I just did one! Forty-some years later I still cannot wait for anything or anyone else.

---

4   http://en.wikipedia.org/wiki/Singapore
5   http://en.wikipedia.org/wiki/Kandang_Kerbau_Women%27s_and_Children%27s_Hospital

Over the centuries the Peranakans (Baba culture) have evolved a unique culture that maintains many Chinese traditions while adopting the customs of the land they settled in as well as their successive colonial rulers. There are traces of Portuguese, Dutch, British, Malay and Indonesian influences in Baba culture.

By the middle of the Twentieth century, most Peranakan were English educated, as a result of the British colonization of Malaya, and the natural propensity of these people who were able to easily embrace new cultures.[6]

Statue of Thomas Stamford Raffles by Thomas Woolner, erected at the spot where he first landed at Singapore. He is recognized as the founder of modern Singapore[7].

---

6   http://en.wikipedia.org/wiki/Peranakan
7   http://en.wikipedia.org/wiki/Singapore

Malaysia

My memory of the story begins in Bukit Besi—Bukit means hill, besi means iron ore or metal. The little jungle village where I grew up was one of three iron ore mining towns owned by a Swiss gentleman. My father was the first Asian physician to work for such a company in Southeast Asia. He left a surgical residency in Kuala Lumpur for this job and, though it is a little bit of a harmful precedent in some ways -the moving around and the gypsy feet. I am ever thankful that he did because it was an idyllic location in the middle of the world and yet apart from it. As I think back today I can, occasionally, get a whiff of that environment which I grew up in and within which I felt very comfortable. As I write today and summer is upon us I can recall the stifling heat when nothing, not even the air, would move. Even a fly or mosquito outside the mosquito netting flying about would be extremely interesting because the heat would penetrate your very core and make the thought of movement or activity such a superhuman requirement and effort that it was certainly not worth it.

Malaysia has always been an interesting place depicted by many different authors (Anthony Burgess, Joseph Conrad, Herman Melville, Robert Louis Stevenson) and discovered by many people. Simply looking at the origins of the names of places I lived has been an interesting and educational exercise. Lanjut means "continuous." Looking at it now, on the Internet, it has evolved into a fascinating travel destination taking advantage of its natural beauty and charms. On the Internet the pristine nature of its beaches and coastline and the landscape that lends easily to gorgeous golfing terrain is captured in full view. It is truly a place that goes on and on. It is continuous. Kuala Lumpur (K. L.) is a combination of two words with Kuala meaning an "estuary or confluence of rivers" and Lumpur meaning, "mud." Ulu Klang, the neighborhood my family lived in when my family lived in K. L., which was at that time far removed from the city and its cement, means "wild place." Both of these names are steeped in the historical origins of the two places.

In my personal history I still remember my first day of school. It was in Bukit Besi where I grew up. Bukit, in Malay, means hill and besi means iron ore. This was a small iron ore-mining town that may have numbered a few thousand people. As I mentioned previously my father was the physician for the Eastern Mining and Metals Company which owned several iron ore mines in eastern Malaysia; the state of Trengannu. I was taken to school by Miriam, one of the amahs (a Malay word which means female servant, even though she and the other amahs were more mamas than amahs to me). At lunch-time she would bring my lunch. It was a one-room schoolhouse taught by an Australian couple, Mr. and Mrs. Smythe. I never knew their first names. My sister went to school there also for four years before me. On my first day of school I ran away and was carried back kicking and screaming by Mrs. Smythe. I did the kicking and screaming. Although I still wonder whether she would not have wanted to kick and scream a little bit having to deal with the likes of me. I am sorry Mrs. Smythe wherever you are now. For as long as I can remember school has always felt that way to me. Through high school, undergraduate college, and medical school. Twenty years of wanting to run away and do my own thing but having something force me back despite an overwhelming urge to kick and scream. In more recent years—the last nineteen or so—that someone has been me.

Our house in Bukit Besi had been a hospital for the Japanese army during World War Two. It was not a big hospital but it was a huge house. I do not know the extent of the remodeling done under my father's direction before I was born but I remember each and every room in that house where I grew up. I remember the deck on the back of the house, the papaya tree and rambutan trees in the back yard, the small swimming pool in the back yard, the tennis court in the front yard, the sandbox beside the house, and the one hundred cement steps down to the hospital that my father had had built below the house.

Malaysia was a fun place for a child to grow up. I spent my days outside running around. Sometimes playing with my soldiers, sometimes with the other children in town, and, more often than not, simply by myself. It was warm—most would say unbearably hot—in the tropics and I never seemed to be able to hang on to a pair of shoes. I ran around barefoot everywhere I went. At one point when I was six or seven years old my father decided that he would no longer buy me any more new shoes because I kept losing them. I did not miss them.

We originally lived in a small iron-ore mining town in the middle of the mountains and jungles of the eastern state of Trengannu. My father was the first, and for many years the only, non-European physician of any of the European companies in this part of Southeast Asia. He had come there after World War Two and the partition of India into India, Pakistan, and, ultimately, Bangladesh. After initially beginning a surgical residency in Kuala Lumpur, the capital of Malaysia, he received an invitation to take a job as the physician for three mining towns in eastern Malaysia—Bukit Besi, Bukit Ibam, and Lanjut. The only routes to these mining towns from Kuala Lumpur, more commonly known as K. L., was by small airplane, by locomotive train through the jungle, or by mountainous, jungle-enveloped roads. It was that way even when I was growing up there in Malaysia. This made each and every trip, of which we took several, from coast to coast an adventure. I remember the train rides we took if for nothing else but for the 'clickety-clack' of the rails and the ever-changing and interesting activity in the deep jungle. As the physician my father took it upon himself to arrange for clearing of much of the local jungle and swampland—which served as a breeding ground for mosquitoes and continual hotbed of malaria for the local populace. Once it was cleared a large field was created and used for a football (what is known in America as soccer) field, a country club where the upper echelons of the mining company and their families were able to dine, play billiards and darts, watch a weekly movie, and, with the adjoining swimming pool, swim.

I learned how to swim in that pool. It was one of my first lessons in life. I had been afraid of the water and hesitant to jump into the pool. One day as I was walking along the edge of the pool with my father by my side he pushed me into the pool. Instead of drowning, I swam. I now associate death with the feeling of being surrounded by water and seeing the air and surface far above. I suppose in many ways it is a peaceful feeling and what I have always felt would be a serene way of passing out of this life. The moments before I went into the water are more frightful and worrisome to me. I have for many years associated those moments and that terror with life. Walking along with a person you trust more than anyone in the world and then within moments having them push you in front of an oncoming locomotive. Still it was a good lesson in life. To quote one of the attending surgeons on my third year surgery clerkship at Monmouth Medical Center during medical school, "you can't trust nobody, no way, no how, not even your mother." This all sounds very harsh and, in truth, it was that same person's insight that led to one of my greatest joys—swimming and the peacefulness of the water.

I learned several things from this experience. I learned that I loved swimming and continued it as a sport and for fun for much of my young days. I learned that when I found something that I could do on my own—swimming—I was extremely happy. Nobody else could interfere or even wanted to. It turns out that my father is deathly afraid of the water and was told as a youngster by a gypsy that he would die someday by drowning. This was the beginning of my discovery of personal independence. I also learned that all things were not what they appeared to be—appearances could be very deceiving. Someone whom you thought would never do anything to hurt you might suddenly do something that they believed was in your best interests despite what you believed to be in your best interests. The only way to have things your way would be to have things your way.

Somewhere in this life-lesson I learned that what is never tried is never known. Once I was forced to try swimming I loved it. In retrospect I am very thankful for the opportunity. We made several moves in Malaysia. At one point we moved to Lanjut, which was on the east coast of Malaysia.

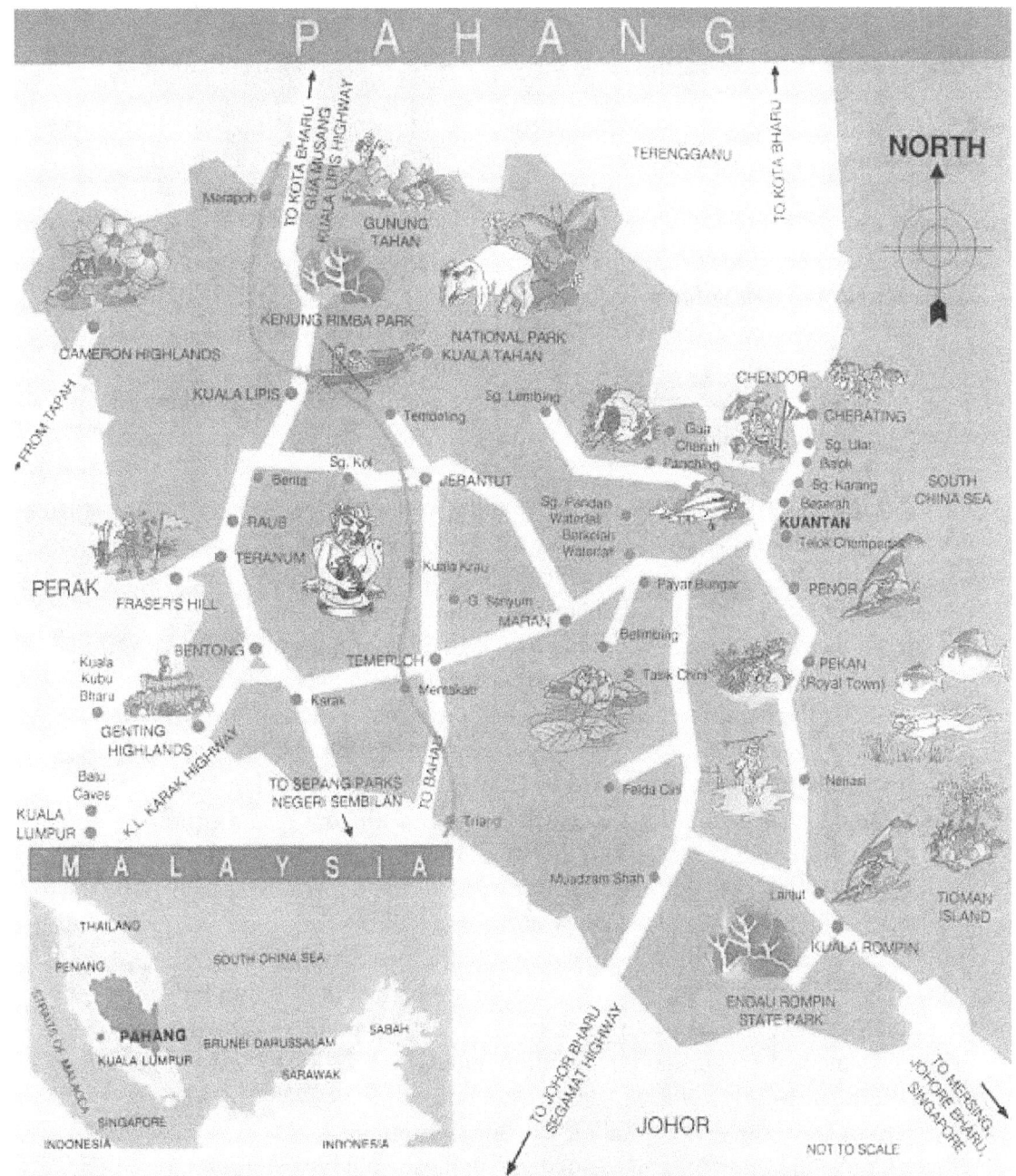

[1] A Map of Malaysia showing Lanjut, Pahang

Our house was one hundred yards from the beach and the South China Sea. This was a wonderful place to live. The air with the scent of the sea and the constant, hypnotic sound of the surf. My daily routine became getting up out of bed, running down to the beach and playing in the surf, and progressing down to the club where there was a swimming pool replenished daily by water from the ocean. I swam there all day and then repeated the process back to the house later in the day. I do not remember much about school here so it must have truly been a wonderful life!

Interestingly, the Arabic honorific of Pahang[2]—the state in Malaysia where Lanjut is located—is *Darul Makmur* ("Abode of Tranquility"). And that it is, in my memory and in the scenes depicted on the internet in travel brochures.

We lived here only briefly but I demonstrated another birthright—the ability to get into trouble, or at least to get everybody else into trouble. I think one of my children has something similar to this—maybe all of them—because my wife and I are always in trouble related to his activities and things he does (well, maybe not, we just think we are in trouble, he does not. So maybe it is our problem and not actually a problem at all).

Later in our stay in Lanjut I learned another important lesson. There was a river inlet several miles away from town with a road through the jungle paralleling the coastline. One day I decided it would be interesting to walk down there for fun and convinced several of my friends and their younger siblings in the area to go with me. We all went and did not decide to turn around to come back home until it was beginning to get dark. Needless to say there were several worried parents back in Lanjut. We, being children, had not informed them of our plans or projected whereabouts. As a parent in today's world I can understand the anxiety generated quite well. As a child in yesterday's world I did not and if I think back to that time I still do not. On our trek back I decided, with a small contingent of our group agreeing with me and following me, that rather than return home along the beach which would take us directly to our back yards it would be better to head inland to the road and walk back that way as someone would come looking for us in a vehicle and we could ride home rather than walk. My intuition proved correct, we rode home while the beach-walking group walked, we got home earlier than the other group, and we did not get into trouble with our parents. I learned that I could trust my inborn instincts to make decisions and that I could make good decisions that worked to my and my compatriots' benefit.

Later we moved to the capital city, Kuala Lumpur, or K. L. There we lived in a suburb known in Malay as 'Ulu Klang,' which means wild place. It was a very well-to-do suburb and away from the hustle and bustle of the city; out in the beginnings of the wildness of the jungle outside the city. These places, Bukit Besi and Lanjut, in the midst of the jungle and all its trees, and the Ulu Klang, outside the city at the edge of the jungle, formed my love of the quiet suburbs away from the city. Of course, it shielded me from all the life, activity, and interesting changes within the city. I would learn about this much later while living in Philadelphia.

When we moved to K. L. it was after we had visited America in the mid-sixties. My father had gone to school in Philadelphia and his best friend from the mining company in Malaysia was a graduate of Stanford. We had visited Palo Alto and my father could see that the best future for his children would be in this land of opportunity. Unfortunately, at that time, and until 1969–70, Asians were not allowed to migrate to the United States of America. Still that was my father's plan. Initially, in K. L. I had gone to the Alice Smith School, a very British, and very prim and proper English school. After my father had set his sights on America as our future home, my sister and I went to the International School of Kuala Lumpur (I.S.K.L.) which was an American school run by Americans. I began to learn about the 'discovery' of America by Christopher Columbus—"Columbus sailed the ocean blue in 1492"—and the basics of American history as they were printed in the sixties. History always enthralled me but there always seemed to be more—"the rest of the story" as Paul Harvey says—as I would find out later in life.

Moss Co.

In 1869 the first settlers came to the area of Idaho now known as Moscow. This name—Moscow—pronounced as in the title to this chapter—was chosen because of its meaning, "city of brotherly love.[8]" Samuel Neff, the postman who ultimately had to choose the official name was born in Moscow, Pennsylvania and later lived in Moscow, Iowa[9]. He was not Russian.

In late 1969 we moved to Moscow, Idaho, the town where Bing Crosby, according to a rumor that I remember hearing at the time, grew up, but from what I could tell, never lived. It snowed here during the winter and I had never seen snow before. I can think of several comments I could make about snow having grown up in the tropics and being quite happy to live wearing shorts, and shirts and shoes only when forced. I will not say any of those things here. Suffice it to say the environment had changed significantly. I did my best to adapt and now thirty or so years later I believe I have begun to do so. We lived in an apartment, which was within walking distance of the public school where I went to sixth and seventh grade. I grew up speaking 'The Queen's English' and yet at Moscow Public School I was getting barely passing grades in English. I also found that none of the sports I grew up playing, like football, i.e., soccer, rugger, cricket, or rounders, translated well to the sports played in America—football, i.e., American football, baseball, and basketball. Still, I tried each sport and after a season playing each discovered that I did not care for any of them. This was all a part of a transformation that can be simplified into the change from calling the last letter of the alphabet zed to calling it zee. That seems so simple and yet, in actuality, it is most difficult. In retrospect, here is a grand life lesson. What may be extremely simple to speak of doing can be the most difficult to actually do.

Swimming pools—swimming having been my biggest and most favorite sport in Malaysia—were very different. I was used to the ocean and the pools at the club, filled with ocean water, where I was one of the few people that swam there. I never got used to the idea of all those people swimming in the same pool and the large number of children urinating in a pool, or so I thought having heard some children bragging about it at one of the public pools, where I was going to swim. I suppose it was okay for the fish to do it, but other people—no! This too was part of a process of learning. Learning to live among a throng of people as opposed to living in the jungle where orangutans, chimpanzees, various monkeys, and other creatures of

---

8   http://en.wikipedia.org/wiki/Moscow,_Idaho
9   ibid

the forest outnumbered us. I am still adjusting to this disparity and am not yet convinced that where I live now is more civilized or safer than where I lived then.

America was a very different place from where I grew up. There were people everywhere—and at that time there weren't as many people as there are now—there was cement everywhere and everybody knew what was on television and when. It seemed that everyone I met knew about everything there was to know that was important and I did not seem to know anything. Living and growing up in the mountainous jungle regions of Malaysia did not prepare me too well for cement, television, public swimming pools, and all the activities of modern American life in the 1970s. Somewhere within all of this was a lesson. A lesson far more useful than Goethe's "what does not kill me, makes me stronger." That may very well be true in this and many situations but kids from the jungles of Malaysia simply do not thrive on brutality of vision or thought. It would seem that that sort of mentality would fit better in an environment like America in the modern, cement, public pool age. In looking back I believe the lesson was that all that occurs in the outer world like the changes from jungle to cement do not mandate changes within. The boy from the Malaysian jungle still survives in thought and in spirit. The best day of one's life is today and, as my four year old always says, tomorrow never comes.

Robin K. Dhillon, M.D., M.B.A.

Spokaloo

I went to eighth, ninth, and tenth grade in Spokane, Washington which was originally incorporated as "Spokan Falls;" named after the Native American tribe that originally lived here—the Spokane Indians or "Children of the Sun." Not surprisingly like much of the country in the North the sun was not an overly prominent component of the daily environs, in direct contrast to Malaysia and Singapore. Once again it was a change in environment before I had yet understood the last environment. The adjustment here involved a more transient community amongst a community of old settlers of the Pacific Northwest. I did not understand life and the inhabitants here and am not convinced that I do yet.

It was not until much later that I discovered that although I was under the mistaken impression that Moscow was somehow related to the upbringing of Bing Crosby, he was actually born in Tacoma, Washington and when he was three years old, in 1906, his family moved to Spokane, Washington[10]. This did have some precedent as noted in Wikipedia, The Free Encyclopedia: "It should be noted that Bing Crosby had no birth certificate and that his birth date was shrouded in mystery until his childhood Roman Catholic church in Tacoma, Washington, released the baptismal records that revealed his date of birth[11]." I must admit that I knew this then, forgot it for many years, and re-learned it while researching this chapter. It is the beauty and the nightmare of Multiple Sclerosis. Forgetting so much that learning the same things one already knows can be a completely new experience, at least until one realizes that one's already been there.

Here I met my first great friend in life—Andy Dallas We were friends from the beginning. Many years later I would find that we were still friends. That all by itself has been a wonderful lesson. Who would have known before the fact. After a recent experience driving down Division Street (a very well traveled thoroughfare) with him driving, seated next to his wife, and my wife and myself in the backseat. On the way out to dinner, one of those cinematic flashbacks occurred. We were all older in appearance but Andy Dallas was still driving down a busy street talking a mile a minute, going exactly the speed limit, aware of all the traffic around, and looking us in the eye as he spoke. As long as I can remember knowing him, from age fourteen to now, he has done this. It is unnerving if you do not know him and amusing if you do. Once again it shows how life and people can stay the same and still change.

---

10   http://en.wikipedia.org/wiki/Bing_Crosby
11   ibid

Here I learned about Chief Joseph and the Nez Perce tribe. As is often the case under the surface there is always more fascinating history. At the same time I learned that I had, only recently, in Idaho walked the same ground that some incredibly interesting figures in history had walked, like Chief Joseph, famous for the words that cinematographers have used but never improved upon when he said, "From today forward I will fight no more." Once again learning echoes life. History seems to parallel individual lives.

My new sport in Spokane became track and field. I ran the four hundred and forty yard dash. This is a race that is somewhere between a sprint like the 100- and 220-yard dashes and the long distance races like the 880-yard and 1 mile run. It did not seem to quite fit with the rest of the events and nobody wanted to take it on. Once again I had found my forté outside the glamour and the glitz. Neither existed with this event. It was more an event that I could do on my own without anyone else trying to horn in on it. In fact, most everybody else did not want to have anything to do with it.

Cold Facts

I finished high school in Colfax, Washington and commuted daily to the state college, Washington State University, sixteen miles away for four years.

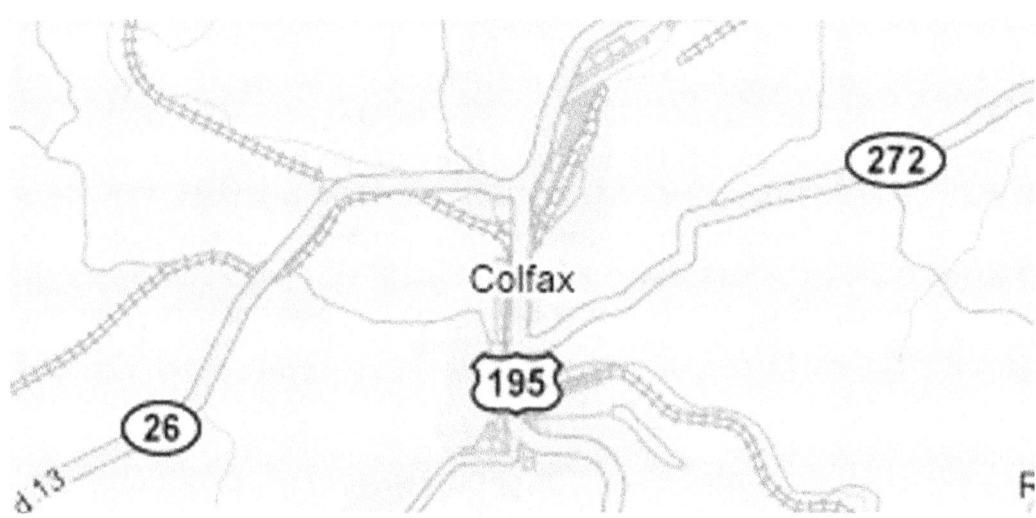

Map of Colfax, WA per Mapquest

Colfax

I initially moved here to live with my father who had a general medical practice there. It was his idea that I leave Spokane and live with him in Colfax. Once again I was an outsider. Only now I was an outsider who, despite not knowing anyone, was known by everyone. I was the new doctor's son. As a teenager I missed the significance of these facts. It is only now that I have begun to understand why I never had too many friends in this small community. Once again the best of intentions were directed at someone else's ideas of my needs rather than my actual needs. It was a lot like learning how to swim.

A Picture of Colfax, Washington (from the town web-site)

During high school I was told that this high school was exceptional because of the high level of education available to students. As was my fashion, I accepted what I was told as fact and did not look at reality which I seem to have done more now in my early dotage than ever before. During high school I took a full course—two years' worth—in accounting on my own and had to do mathematics by myself with just the textbook for a teacher because I had advanced beyond what they were teaching in that school. Now, for the individual, like most Americans, confronted by this situation with the proximity of institutes of higher learning, would have taken advanced courses at one of those universities so as not to waste their intellectual effort. I did not. Instead I listened to the school counselor who advised me to stay in high school rather than graduate early and go on to college. Once again, it seemed here was another lesson. Today I am convinced that the lesson was far more important than what I might have gained by getting out of high school a year early and starting college. As the Buddhists say, "the journey of a thousand steps, begins with one step." I would add to that that with each step and placement of one foot then the other, the journey's final destination changes. If, somehow, I had made different steps then, I would not be where I am now. I realize now that where I am now is where I want to be. They used to call that blind dumb luck! Probably, more appropriately, I would consider it Divine Providence (though I am not certain that it is directed at me, specifically, but, rather is directed at all of us here on this earthly plane).

I worked on a farm during the summers. A job my father arranged for me with a patient of his who was a farmer. I liked the work but I did not much care for the extra arrangements that got me the job. It was not exactly an exclusive job and there were many to be had in the area. So, on the one hand, it would not have been too difficult for me to get such a job without my father being involved and, on the other hand, with my father making the introductions, etcetera, it was his initiative and to his credit that I worked at all. It was another lesson. When you take those first steps going from crawling to walking you never make the transition if someone is always holding your hand or supporting you in some way. Still, my employment on the farm and going to a state university allowed me to pay for my undergraduate education when I went to college. Compared to the costs of a large part of my education, like medical school, all underwritten by my father, this was miniscule but it taught me something. It taught me that what I did for myself and what I accomplished based on my own effort was mine and mine alone. It was like swimming and running the 440-yard dash. When I got done, I could be satisfied that I had done well and that in visualizing a difference between crawling and walking I would walk.

During the time I studied at Washington State University located in Pullman, Washington.

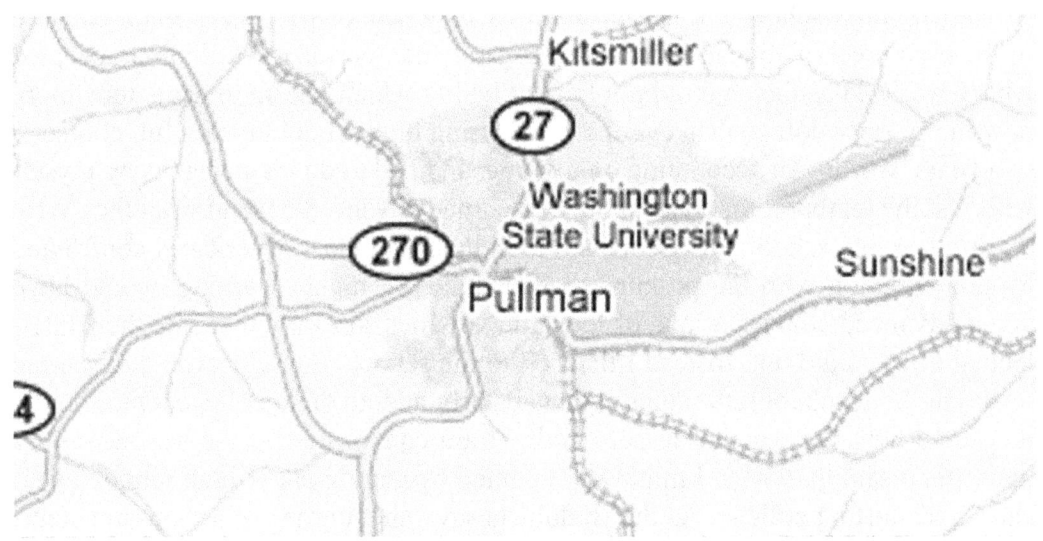

Map of Pullman, WA per Mapquest

I began my studies much as I begin just about everything I have done in life in a very gung-ho fashion. My enthusiasm never fizzled it simply became redirected during the course of four years of study in Pullman at W. S. U. When I began I had classes that began at seven in the morning so I would have to get up very early to shower and then make the half hour drive from Colfax to Pullman. By my final semester I am not certain if I made it to classes except for the first day and test days. I did make it to the Compton Union Building (C. U. B.) daily where I could shoot pool and play pinball machines incessantly. I wasn't that good at either of them but I imagined myself to be far better accomplished than I was. With my imagination running rampant it all seemed okay. Not only did I shoot a mean game of pool but also I could maneuver those pinball machines very deftly. I played them deftly enough that they would always accept another quarter from me to play another game. I also learned to play foosball which is a game designed for drunks in bars and college campuses, of which there are two in the area, which seem to have been developed around collections of drinking establishments.

I graduated from Washington State University with a Bachelor of Science degree in Biology in 1980. That is what I was told all premedical students did by my advisor at the university. It is only now that I understand that advisors' advice is worth what you pay for it—nothing in this case. I did not get accepted to the only medical school I applied to at that time—the University of Washington. They viewed themselves as the Harvard of the West and I did not fit their self-styled vision of a 'Harvard medical student.' I should have applied to Harvard, I would have fit their model and vision.

I did not get into medical school largely due to my own naiveté and the lack of an experienced voice—experienced in how I would be able to achieve the goals I desired—and useful advice. I was convinced that Medicine was the right field for me to pursue. A large part of that was related to what I had directly observed of my father while we lived together in Colfax. He had a great respect for the profession of Medicine and his role as a physician. His view of a physicians' role, which harkened back to days of yesteryear when the doctor was not only one who treated physical ailments but also emotional and other more ethereal conditions, struck a resonant chord with me. I watched him carefully as he never had a pager or an answering service yet the hospital and his patients could always find him. When so much in life, especially today, is fluid and changing, he was a constant in his patients' lives. He delivered their babies, gave their babies their shots before school began, fixed their children's fractures, took out their diseased gallbladders, and visited their ailing parents at their homes if they needed a blood pressure check or, simply, a warm hand and the warmth of a good friend's visit. As in later years, the Malay in me responded. It was a good thing to help so many people in so many ways.

As I was convinced that Medicine was to be the path I would follow, I could not envision the many approaches that others had taken to getting into medical school. Graduate studies or joining the workforce with yearly reapplications to medical school and expanding the number of schools I applied to did not appeal to me. One day I saw an advertisement for a medical school in Guadalajara, Mexico. I had heard about this school and that it was easier to gain acceptance than schools in America. As my time to graduation was rapidly approaching I applied there and was rewarded by a prompt response informing me that I had an interview at The Autonomous University of Guadalajara School of Medicine in Guadalajara, Jalisco, Mexico.

When I was nineteen years old I lost most of my hair and rapidly developed what they call 'male-pattern baldness.' As a result, since that time I have appeared older than I am—twenty years old looking like forty. My reaction to that has always been, "oh, well...I yam what I yam." My forebears are Sikhs. Sikhs are members of a distinct monotheistic religious group in Northern India who, in their origins in the 1400s, developed certain distinctive attributes to set themselves apart from the multitude of religions in India and to facilitate their identification and association with each other. One of those markers, for men, was that they never cut their hair. As a result all the men have extremely long hair, which they take great care to groom and wear tidily under a turban. Once again, it seems, I was separated from the mainstream by a natural turn of events. Herein lay one more lesson. I learned a great deal in reading about Sikhism and have a profound respect for it as a great religion and system of nonviolent thought, which came about in the midst of very violent times. Still each individual's life seems to be molded by circumstances which direct our feet along that 'journey of a thousand steps,' but who knows which thousand steps? My steps took me out of the country, to Guadalajara.

The Guad Squad

My father, to his credit, insisted that his children go to medical school. Although I have an older brother and sister, I ended up being the only one to go. To go there I ended up going to what has been called "the most Mexican city in Mexico," Guadalajara. It is depicted on the Guadalajara web site much as it is in reality.

The central square in Guadalajara, Jalisco, Mexico[3]

I ended up going there for many reasons not the least of which was that I was not all that cocksure in my presentation and quite reserved (at least that is what I decided in hindsight which, as I would learn years later, is always 20-20[4], i.e., perfect vision). I didn't talk much. As I had been growing up I spent more time listening and, thus, was much more influenced by other's thoughts and ideas. In that I am thankful to the times during which I grew up, my parents who directed that environment, the amahs, and so many more who now seem unseen and forgotten in my memory. The word Guadalajara comes from the Arab word "Wad-al-hidjara", which means "River that runs between rocks". The city is named after the native city of Nuño Beltrán de Guzmán, the discoverer of Guadalajara[5].

Of the 10,000 Americans in foreign medical schools approximately 2%, or 200, transfer out into American schools every four years. They would have graduated from an American medical school if they had been accepted there in the first place. These numbers are much lower today as Medicine as a profession rapidly becomes less financially lucrative. Certainly people have far less respect for physicians today than when Midas Welby was a doctor. In those days it was Midas Welby, M. D. Today it is Might as Well be an M. D. Or, stated another way, M. D. today seems to stand for Mental Deficient. Who else would work twenty four hours a day, seven days a week, get paid less and less with each passing week, and have everyone treat them as if they earned more than they deserved anyhow? In other words, today doctors seem to be walking around and saying "Please, pay me less, let me work harder than any other human being around, call me names, if you wish, don't pay my bill..." I am certain there is a different litany for every physician out there today.

In the Fall of 1980, I went to Guadalajara, Mexico for my interview to get into medical school and to begin a journey which amazes me while I look back on it even though I lived it. When I walked into the interview I was seated at a conference table. Soon thereafter in walked someone who was obviously an American, and a student, by the way he was dressed. It turned out that they were interviewing both of us at the same time. That was a day that will live on in my memory. He and I became the best of friends; like twin brothers from different parents and different worlds. We are friends today. Our wives are friends. Our children are friends. As for our friends...we haven't tested that yet.

I later realized that I had lived my childhood with an elaborate set of protective shields in place. I rarely spoke and even less frequently let on what I was thinking or what was going on in my mind. Years after my experience in Mexico—my first experience of living on my own—I realized that I had lived in a very protective environment. Not just by my own shields but also by all those around me making decisions for me, which I, today, insist that my children make for themselves. Now the shields are down.

Americans at UAG

Our house, was a place where everyone except the cocaine-smuggling Colombian got away—Juan Moore Ghai, Ron Kahn Dawn, Harry Trees: we started out with an ivy league jock house-mate who ended up being cast off and out because of competition which was more imagined than real.

My friend taught me many things that I have found to be true over the course of life. Many of these life lessons were passed down from his father and mother who, having had twelve children proved to be parents who should have had <u>twelve</u> children. Juan always told me the story of how his parents met and the lessons they imparted to him about true love. It was why he and Angel, he believed, would always be together. They were very different with him being a very "angular" Americano cut from the old conservative Ivy League mold. He walked, talked, dressed, and lived like "a doctor." Angel was very proud of her Native Mexican or Indian heritage. Her father was a very pure "Indio de Mexico" (Mexican Indian). As straight-laced as Juan was, Angel was the opposite. They married in Mexico, had two children, and are together today. Having lived an exposure to true love, true learning, true life

The true love came in the way of my two great friends—Angel Del Sur & Juan Moore Ghai. They met purely by chance. On the first day of classes at the Medical School at "Universidad Autonoma de Guadalajara" they were assigned seats nest to each other and the rest, as is often claimed, is history. They have not stop talking (or, depending on their mood at the moment, fighting) ever since. Although many years later I met my Sweet Gaelic Breeze and I recreated much of what I had learned from this experience it was truly what was ideal in both of their minds and conversations with me that I was able to recognize how this Sweet Gaelic Breeze was truly my perfect match.

The true learning, as I like to call the Juan Moore Ghai method, was relatively simple. Simplicity has always been appealing to me and from what I have since seen in Surgery and in life seems to be the underpinning to much of existence. Simple things seem to work as I witnessed many years previously in farming. If things flowed smoothly they usually worked and went quite well. This way of thinking, acting, and being seemed to work quite well for much of what later developed. Placing chest tubes successfully, making coronary anastomoses that conducted blood efficiently and effectively without leaking, opening and closing various wounds, removing lung tumors, and so much more was molded around simplicity. His method simply involved working hard, i.e., read as much as you can, summarizing the important points succinctly, briefly, and in your own words (almost writing your own book on what you read and heard) and repeating these things you learned as often as possible (actually, more often than that). It was simple. Be complete. Write it all down. Repeat. Repeat. Repeat…as I would hear many times later, "Not just Pete, but Re-Pete."

The essence of much of what went on involved what I can only describe as the true life. As I would learn with time this involved placing Ron Kahn Dawn, or myself, on his own. It was not something that was consciously planned. It just happened. I told myself later that although much of what I did had been done by others even though not many were able to do it; it had been done before.

So much of this ended up becoming a mélange of character traits that together were the art of learning. It involved experience as a subjective, first-person activity rather than as someone else's story. It became my own life, with my own friends, like Juan Moore Ghai, Angel Del Sur, Andy Dallas, and My Sweet Gaelic Breeze. While I was in Mexico I learned many things. As in college starting out very seriously going to all the 7 a. m. classes in the beginning and spending all my time either in class, in the library, or at home with a book. I later learned about pinball machines, foosball tables, pool tables, beer, live music, and girls. In Mexico I learned about the Basic Medical Sciences, Physical Examination, History-taking, Spanish, Mexico, shooting nine-ball for pennies, eating "tacos en la calle," and, tequila. I not only drank cheap, rotgut tequila, I drank very fine tequila, I learned how it was made, and I worked for the people who made it in a little "pueblo" called "Tequila." In the end the experience taught me about living for the present day, not for some future day. After two and a half years of living in Mexico I did the unthinkable—I drank the water. It was good. I didn't get sick.

To be able to transfer out of Mexico into an American Medical School an interesting rite had been concocted. This rite involved taking an examination that was more difficult than any exam that medical students in American Schools ever had to take. Students who did well on these exams were then invited by American medical schools to join their schools taking positions that students had vacated for various and sundry reasons. As they paid very dearly for their schooling with family funds, loans, or Government/Military support it was a fund drain for the schools and usually an involuntary act on the part of the student. The exam I had to take was called "The Medical Sciences Knowledge Profile" or M.S.K.P. I took it in Mexico City on the top floor of a hotel during an earthquake. In a fashion I rock 'n rolled through it!

I didn't know it at the time but I was on my way to going away and getting out of this boondoggle of being in a foreign medical school and graduating from it becoming one of the largely disparaged and shunned "F.M.G.'s." Along the way

I spent six months in Seattle studying followed by six months auditing medical school classes in Pathology at U.S.C. (the University of Solid Cash). I received a solicitation in the mail to apply to Hahnemann School of Medicine. I sent it in a week after the deadline. Much to my surprise two weeks later I was accepted into Hahnemann. They required me to repeat half a year.

Soon thereafter much like Dorothy in <u>Through The Looking Glass</u> I was off to see the wizard.

The City of Love

Soon I moved to Philadelphia. I learned quite quickly that the city was known as "the city of brotherly love." Of course my first exposure to the city of brotherly love was after getting an apartment on Benjamin Franklin Parkway where the school told me that many of the medical students stayed. It was smack-dab in the middle of downtown Philadelphia. This was what was known as "center city." It was all city, a far cry from the jungle where I grew up, but a jungle nonetheless. My first night there I tried to sleep and was awoken, despite being on the 9th floor by a loud voice. This voice belonged to one of the inhabitants of this new jungle. The screamer. Every night he walked through the city screaming at the top of his lungs something that, try as I might, I was never able to decipher. I spent many nights watching out the window looking to see who this poor fellow in so much pain and distress was. As with so many things I was persistent. Finally, one night I saw him. He was very tall and strode more than he walked. He scared me <u>and</u> inspired me. He was very large and very angry. This scared me. Yet he was very serious about so much. About whatever he was angry about and wherever it was that he was going. He never gave up.

When I first started school there I spent at least the first two weeks walking on air finally I regained access to the gravitational pull of the earth and landed back on the ground. Once back into reality I looked around and was able to finally take a close look at all the people who had had what I had wanted from the very beginning and what I desired, as did many others at "Guad," for so many years (granted it was only <u>two</u> years but it seemed like a really long time back then). After careful observation I noticed something quite peculiar. The people at Hahnemann were exactly the same as those at "Guad."

Quickly as I noticed that I was seeing those same people around me in Philadelphia as I had seen in Guadalajara I returned back to "the grind," learning every day.

Homeopathy was discovered and developed by Dr. Samuel Hahnemann[12], one of the great geniuses in the history of medicine. Dr. Hahnemann learned fourteen languages in order to read every medical text available in Germany in the late 1700's. His discovery of the fundamental principles of Homeopathic Medicine occurred when he was in his forties in the 1790's. He continued to practice, write, and teach until his death in 1843 at the age of 88 years. This was the foundation of the School of Medicine at Hahnemann University yet most if not all of the students in Philadelphia were quite unaware of this background. My biggest discovery in this time was that the same kids in school here were in Guad. only not as experienced, worldly, or as motivated as the motivated students at Guad. "The House of God[13]" finally made sense.

One of the crowning moments in medical school for me was at the end of my Psychiatry rotation (in which I was permitted to take the final exam twice having failed the first time) was a walk in the park—the medical students, the nurse assistants, the nurses, and the patients from the thirty-day ward out for a walk in center city. There were other people there—imaginary people. The best part of it all was that I ultimately trained in Surgery and then the apotheosis of surgical subspecialties—Cardiothoracic Surgery—and without a directed effort was able to fail the ultimate form of non-practical fields, i.e., Psychiatry. There are Surgeons and there are Psychiatrists both reputedly at opposite ends of the spectrum in terms of personality and approaches.

This chapter could just as easily have been titled "East coast bagels, bakeries, and bagmen." These are among the many elements that seemed to be evanescent in

---

12   http://www.lycos.com/info/homeopathy--samuel-hahnemann.html
13   The House of God: The Classic Novel of Life and Death in an American Hospital by Samuel Shem, M.D.—a book that all interested in Medicine, and especially Surgery, should read.

East coast cities. I discovered this while living in Philadelphia without a car (cars being ubiquitous on the West coast and quite impossible to live without). As a result I walked to and from school and, essentially, everywhere I wanted to go. This didn't include much besides school and my apartment. Still it did include at least one St. George's Diner (for some reason they were all named after St. George. I guess he really liked Philly Cheese-Steaks or the wonderful coffee they made in those diners. Or maybe he had become the patron saint of East coast diners?

Regardless, in walking everywhere I went into the bakeries as the smells wafting out the doors not only proceeded heavenward but also were heavenly. The bagels and baked goods were like none to be had outside of the East coast.

I also met many of the people who lived on the street. Much like those I met in the tropics if one was kind and pleasant to them they returned the same attitude. It would get extremely cold in winter and now, while I have time to think, I wonder how they survived. Much as I do pay homage to the many brave and courageous soldiers who have and continue to protect us I paid homage to all those who ran shelters for the homeless, soup kitchens, and the like. It is truly humbling to know that people like that exist out there. Yet what is even more humbling is to actually see and talk to people living in such dire conditions. Possibly it is a protective mechanism for the majority of human beings to believe all these people are somehow different or lesser than oneself. In talking to them I found that often times they were no different from all the other people around. They just didn't have homes and support groups. I distinctly remember having one fellow with his clothing stuffed with newspapers who stopped me by standing in front of me, caught my eye, and rattled of a name, then concluded by saying, "He was a member of the British parliament in 1867. Look it up." I looked it up. He was.

After three and a half years I completed the course of study and was set to graduate from medical school. As I detail in the next chapter this grand transition was also filled with discovery.

Love in the City

The R&R Hall Of Fame, Cleveland, Ohio
(see website reference below)
http://www.greatbuildings.com/buildings/Rock_and_Roll_Hall_of_Fame.html

In what followed I went through what in Medical School is called "The Match." It is an elaborate, computerized system whereby individuals who are 4th-year medical students go to different hospitals around the country and interview with the Attending staff in the specialty they are interested in. after this process is complete the individuals and the programs rank each other and by a computerized system are matched together, hence "The Match." Next I moved to Cleveland...driving through Solon echoing Drew Carey's opening theme only I did not have anyone—yet—that I could have accidentally left in Solon.

My first day was on Hanna House 3, on the First of July, 1986. As I look back I realize I was learning from the outset. As my Gaelic breeze would later say, and always maintained, the hospital was not only a dangerous place it was downright ugly (or as I later learned to recognize it—fugly). All the newly advanced second year residents could not wait to move on and in so doing essentially dumped their patient load and duties on the incoming interns quite unceremoniously. The patients were the incoming residents problem, not the outgoing second-year resident's. People would suffer and die and the only ones left to help them were the nurses. God bless them!

Robin K. Dhillon, M.D., M.B.A.

I started with the Cardiothoracic Surgery service. It was quite scary as it was always busy and the patients were quite sick. On top of it all things happened very quickly. I discovered that then as now I did not want bad things to happen to people and especially not if I could make it either better or go away. It was why I became a doctor (or, at least, why I had kept going once I was channeled into it by my father). I was busy every night and day with the only help being the nursing staff. At every moment I felt as if I did not know anything. It was like being in a foreign country where nobody spoke your language <u>and</u> the extremes of paranoia were true—everyone really was trying to get you.

Three different hospitals were a part of the surgical training program where I ended up doing my training. The main hospital was University Hospital of Cleveland which had a long storied history, much like its main competitor in town—the Cleveland Clinic. Somewhere long ago in their origins there was a common thread, however that had been lost with time. When I started training in Surgery, the two institutions seemed to follow two different models. Of course, this was simply the perspective of a newcomer on the scene. It all seemed very business-like and concerned with its image and somewhat preoccupied with how it compared to the juggernaut that was The Cleveland Clinic Foundation. The Wade Park Veteran's Administration (WPVA) at that time was a remnant of the classic veteran's hospitals. One could sense a heavy layer of gratitude in the air and yet there seemed to be an added aura of entitlement from what I can only describe as "hangers-on" or "wanna-be's." Many of the Veterans had been injured in the line of duty and suffered then and many suffered for years after their active service. There was much to think about here. In moments of quiet reflection it became quite obvious that this was all about paying back our veterans for the freedom they allowed us. The third hospital in the training program was Cleveland Metropolitan General Hospital (CMGH). It was the county hospital where we were taking care of everyone. It provided hope for even the poorest of the poor.

Many of the simple, early lessons directed at neophytes like myself were powerful lessons and hold true for so many aspects of life. Every step of the way it was reinforced that building a reputation by being honest, generous, caring, and hard-working began on day one and had to be augmented and reinforced every day thereafter. It meant hard work and constant vigilance for long hours. Still, somehow it seemed to be very rewarding. At the end of the day it felt good. What seemed to be difficult for some was that all this effort was directed at somebody else's service and benefit. I was convinced then (and even more now) that even though good surgeons could be selfish, <u>great</u> surgeons could not be. It was (and is) all about the patient.

Then one day in 1987 I ran into A Sweet Gaelic Breeze. She had gone away to stay with her closest friend (they had been friends since early childhood) in Southern Italy. Her friends in the Intensive Care Unit, where she worked knew her well and had come to know me from my work in the hospital that past year. They all thought we should meet. One day we did and after a lot of eye avoidance and indirect directness we finally went on a date. Somewhere in that giddy haze it all became serious—well as serious as a crazy Indian from Southeast Asia and a sweet Irish lass can be.

Dixie

In 1988 it became quite serious. I needed a job to complete surgery training and complete my dream of becoming a Surgeon. The earliest lessons I had leaned were to come into play. The long hours and hard work was noticed; not just by the nursing staff and patients but also by the higher ups in the training program. I had built a reputation of being honest, generous, caring, and hard working. As a result when the Resident Director of the Surgery program I was in moved down South to become the Chief of Surgery in Mississippi I was invited to join his program. I thought long and hard for almost thirty three seconds before saying, "YES! Sign me up."

I loved the Blues and My Sweet Gaelic Breeze (not in that order). I made plans to move and assumed that My Sweet Gaelic Breeze would move happily along with me. At this point it is probably obvious to most (except for those with a Surgical mindset like mine—this is what has to be done to accomplish "x" goal and this is what needs to happen, so "let's ROCK!! Let's GO!!!"). I never even considered that My Sweet Gaelic Breeze would not want to go wherever I was going. Unbeknownst to me her mother, whom she was very close to, told her she needed to go with me and that was the only reason she moved to Mississippi with me. Today, now that I am a Catholic and believe in God as much as He has always believed in me I spend frequent periods of time sending my thought waves on high. Each time I begin with "Thank you, Annette." I hope and pray she hears it as I was always too stubborn to have seen what was right in front of me and by the time I realized that the door He opened after one had closed wasn't a second floor door without stairs leading up but was actually a grander entrance-way than the one that had closed,[6] she was gone.

In early summer, 1988, we moved from Cleveland, Ohio to Jackson, Mississippi. When we first moved we moved into a duplex on the north side of Jackson, Mississippi just off Interstate 55. Initially it was just My Sweet Gaelic Breeze, me, and whatever we had been able to cram into the car—a small Subaru Hatchback—for the drive down. Like Don Quixote, there I went. Everything else, like our bed, went with the movers. So we were sleeping on the floor. The movers brought our stuff six weeks late. For My Sweet Gaelic Breeze it was unfair, I now realize. Although I never slept much when I was on call, I at least had a bed to lie on. I'm slow to catch on to a lot of really big things. My Sweet Gaelic Breeze was alone while I worked. Her sacrifice as always was immense and like so much I think I can never repay that debt but it would be fun to try.

One day, not so long ago, our first child was born. It was a magical event that with her and the two boys since I have always insisted was well worth the nine months of puking and pain. Jokingly I have persistently repeated that I do not know how I did it! In dissecting out the rationale behind my comment I realize now that it was born of jealousy. It was something, along with many other somethings, that My Sweet Gaelic Breeze has always done with grace and style and without thought for herself or her own needs. If I could I would. It is a large part of why I finally came to believe in God and why life, difficult as it may be at times with all the mistakes I am still quite capable of making, is still such a blessing.

Many people—within the hospital and without—have highly preconceived ideas of what surgeons are like. Even within the profession many have a clear-cut idea of who a surgeon is and how a surgeon is supposed to behave. This led to one of our—My Sweet Gaelic Breeze and my—favorite past-times. While sitting in a highly visited area of the hospital such as the cafeteria we would observe people passing by and make up stories about them based on very superficial characteristics. It was quite amusing to us, especially when we would see doctors or nurses and, on reading their hospital badges as they passed by, were able to fairly accurately pinpoint their specialty or focus.

The surgeons marched hurriedly by with their heads down (in a rush to get to the operating room, I guess). The internists always seemed to be lost in thought. They were not very accomplished at the basics of life. I would spot them as the ones who might absent-mindedly trip over things on the floor, mutter, "Excuse me," and move on, lost in thought. Even when what they had tripped over was inanimate. The Pediatricians were the most fun. I remember from as far back as the third year in medical school I had found them to be able to relate to the kids they treated because they enjoyed the same things, were full of fun, and wanted everyone around to enjoy the day. The nurses from the intensive care units were very efficient and organized. Those from the wards appeared very harried (from so many patients) and busy.

And like them, all of life in residency was very busy. Each day involved a plethora of somewhat humdrum duties to ensure the wellbeing of each patient, their preparedness for upcoming surgery, or their safe recovery from surgery already performed. Still every day allowed for discovery of something completely new. It was mostly medical/surgical information but to one like me it made every day seem like a birthday filled with gifts.

One of those gifts, for me after surgical residency, was a daily and powerful depiction of the truth in many of the old proverbs and sayings. The early bird catches the worm (yet I've seen worms, put them on hooks when fishing, and am not certain why it would be, in general, so wonderful to have one?) Still it was always better to be early rather than late. Disease was simpler and easier to eradicate the earlier one caught it and began treating it.

In thoracic surgery residency I learned a few more truths. An open chest with lungs breathing and the heart beating is truly an awe-inspiring event. However, when one holds a sharp knife in one's hand and a true heart surgeon's responsibility in one's heart all this cannot be appreciated until much later in life. There was a great deal of information to collect and master. Forgetting was not an option. As one of my favorite Attendings (or "Pretendings" as we used to call them) would often say, "A short pencil is worth more than a long memory."

With attention to the sensation in one's fingertips one could feel through the surgical instruments where they needed to go. The patient's tissues guided cutting and sewing. To be a good and artful surgeon one needed to follow the directions allowed by the patient's body. It took the refinement of interpreting the five senses in getting to know and treat people to a glorious pinnacle. To do it and do it well required every minute of every day. It was a powerful experience. One could easily see how those who had done it successfully could easily begin to believe that they too could walk on water.

Somehow, in the midst of all this hectic daily schedule, first at the hospital and, then, at home I learned many things. These things I learned from an old friend—My Sweet Gaelic Breeze—and a new friend—Anne Lande. One day years down the road Anne said something that has always stayed with me. She said, "When you do something you love, you don't work a day in your life."

As I think back now, I worked very hard at the hospital and My Sweet Gaelic Breeze worked very hard at home. She understood what I did each day and made it easy for me when I was able to come home. It has always inspired in me a wish to be able to do the same for her.

My other new friend, Anne, was a surgical resident much as I was and became a good friend not only to me but to my wife as well. Of course, there were a few differences. She was from Mississippi. She had been at the training program since day one. She had had another life even before Medical School as an engineer. Not only was she very bright, she was industrious and trustworthy, and, above all, not only a good surgeon but a good doctor as well.

One day—out of a clear blue sky … wham … bam … a-la-ka-zam … our second child was born. As usual, even though I have always claimed to have suffered through nine months of tortuous hellfire and damnation with each of the three children, it truly was amazing and what My Sweet Gaelic Breeze put up with just with daily morning sickness topped off by the pain of labor and all the trials and tribulations since I cannot even imagine. The second time the result was a boy with—as they say down South—"REEEEL RE-ED HAR."

As I think back to those days so long ago the pleasures certainly were simple. I do remember the drive home after being on call. Anywhere from 24 to 36+ hours on call. Most of that time—hopefully—was spent in the operating room. Regardless, everything one did was in preparation for going to the operating room and OPERATING! The call room was purportedly where one slept. Other residents did all sorts of things there and I was glad that housekeeping was kind enough to change the sheets in the room daily. Still I rarely slept even with clean sheets and my eyes closed. No, I spent most of my time reviewing, in my mind, the patients in-house, the surgeries coming up, and anything rattling around my brain (some people call it knowledge and I learned to call it "l'arnin.'") With all the sleep deprivation, the best part of the day was the drive home. As I always maintained, the best part of driving home was watching the sunrise.

I learned something new down South. Crawfish are mighty good! And they were easily obtained, spiced and cooked with a six-pack of beer in the drive-through on the way home. It always led to my favorite question-and-answer session down in Dixie. The people working in the drive through were always so polite. As one was paying for the crawfish and beer they never failed to ask, "Can I pop the top for ya'?" How could I say no. Those beers and the pound or two of medium spicy mudbugs were perfect on the mile or two drive home and while sitting in the driveway before going inside and collapsing on the couch.

When I finished my training despite having traveled the country looking for a job, I didn't find one that agreed with me or that thought that I agreed with them. My chairman, Roger Mars, knew someone at Texas Heart Institute (THI) and needed someone to do heart transplants in his program that was trained specifically to do heart transplants. So off I went with My Sweet Gaelic Breeze and two children in tow.

Being a Heart Transplant fellow was interesting in many ways. However, in the organization at THI at that time there were a few "chiefs" and a great many "Indians," so to speak. Only the "chiefs" were given the opportunity to operate and all the "Indians" served the "chiefs," the patients, and anybody else who happened along. From hero to zero in a short lateral (sideways) move from Jackson, MS to Houston, TX.

I did my best to learn as much as I could, continued a life-long need to do the best that could be done in the role given to me, and keep everyone around happy. I rode my bike to work each day. One day when My Sweet Gaelic Breeze and the two kids were in Cleveland, I woke up late and was feeling a bit lazy. So I drove my Chevy Suburban to work. After work I looked throughout the lot where I had parked in the morning. The truck cost as much as I had earned the entire last year of my fellowship. I never found it. It was gone. Stolen. A memory.

It was the proverbial last straw that encouraged me to leave. My Sweet Gaelic Breeze had lived in Denver before and in my memory seemed to always say wonderful things about it. So I took a job in Denver, Colorado.

What followed was a brief interlude in Denver. Here I was the "low man on the totem pole" and it did not seem as if it was ever going to change. In my mind this scenario set me in motion to the next stop, as I will later describe.

After leaving Denver and then Rapid City, South Dakota I had wanted a respite from all the craziness and returned to the place where I had been happiest. Roger Mars was still there and offered me a position at the University. I was able to combine many of the things I loved best—operating, patient care, and teaching (medical students, residents) with learning (from the patients, the nurses, other physicians). It was too good to be true. Like so much in life, it reminded me of an earlier passion of mine—music. In particular during my days and nights in Colfax I was a fan of Jimi Hendrix. As we moved back to Mississippi, I thought of "Voodoo Chile (Slight Return)."

In keeping with all that had gone before I was filled with wonderful ideas (at least I thought they were wonderful). So I convinced My Sweet Gaelic Breeze, my best friend, Anne Lande, and her husband (Jack), and my sister, Adelle, and her husband (Jeff), to join us in Memphis, TN for our wedding. My friend, Anne, had gone to school there and was very familiar with things like, where to get a beer and the best ribs in town. Jeff and Adelle had always, since my high school days, been ones I had shared all my fun with. My idea was to spend a weekend in Memphis—a town filled with music and good food—enjoy the company of family and friends—and renew our wedding vows by Elvis—the King of Rock and Roll.

At that time Elvis' real name was John. We found this out when we were being picked up in the morning on the day of the ceremony by a trio of characters.

There was "Elvis" (a.k.a. John), his girlfriend, "'cilla," sitting up front with the fellow driving. We sat in the back on either side of "Elvis." The license plate had a silhouette of Elvis Presley and the words, "I'm dead," underneath. As we got in the driver looked at us in the rearview mirror and very seriously said, "This used to be Elvis's car."

In unison we breathed out stupendously, "Really?"

His response to this was, "No. We just tell people that." That started a wonderful weekend after we all celebrated at "The Chapel of Love." Afterwards we went out and had ribs and beer as they can only truly be enjoyed. In Memphis, listening to The Blues, with the company of good friends and family.

The next morning when I awoke my neck was really hurting. It just wouldn't go away and, unlike my usual approach to such things, I wasn't able to ignore it. Somewhere amidst all the fun I realized that something really was wrong. So I spoke to the two people I trusted most (unlike the song it wasn't the Son and the Holy Ghost—that came, unexpectedly, later). At that time it was My Sweet Gaelic Breeze and Anne Lande.

As they both astutely pointed out I had been working daily for several years in Chest Surgery with loupes (magnifying glasses) on. This involved focusing through those loupes on structures that were extremely small—approximately 2-3 millimeters in diameter. Once one focused in, to look away from the magnification ("over the loupes") destroyed one's focus, required refocusing to continue working, and, generally slowed things down. It was essential to minimize the time on the cardio-pulmonary bypass machine and under anesthesia. Both were unnatural and made people quite sick. At any rate I had spent several years locked into that position and a slipped intervertebral disc was not unusual in that situation.

Something didn't seem right, so, as the good doctor, and as I have always done, after my Brain MRI was done, I asked the technicians (who knew me from all my years of residency training and to whom I had always been kind), what they saw. That is how I found out that that there were multiple plaques (scar tissue) on my brain. As I read later—and have done so many times since—this means the diagnosis of Multiple Sclerosis is assured. I didn't realize it right away, but that is what I had.

Have Knife, Will Travel

Taking up the story after training is not complete without outlining the whirlwind tour of America that I conducted. Following training, the next stop in my tour was Houston, Texas, where my Chairman, Roger Mars, had personal connections. At the same time he was eager, as always, to find a role for one of his trainees, in this case, me. I, being the personality that I am, rather reserved and not very talkative—especially about myself and my own accomplishments and abilities—was hardly the typical cardiac surgeon. As a result jobs were difficult to find as few (essentially none) of the prospective employers out there wanted to take a chance on me. My chairman knew my abilities and me. It was a bargain for him and he was able to see an opportunity that he <u>and</u> I could make use of in this difficult situation.

As a result I ended up becoming part of the cadre of Cardiac Transplant Fellows at Texas Heart Institute. The institute and the position were a mouthful. For me it was quite interesting but very far removed from the personalized type of medical care that held my interest. Simply mentioning "Texas Heart Institute" in a sentence, even today, is often associated with an inaudible sigh from anyone listening. It was not for me.

So I moved on to a new opportunity. This was in Denver, Colorado with a pair of surgeons who seemed to be the best of friends. I learned many things here about many things. I learned about life in the big city with people in my field who have dollar signs in their eyes and, in looking back, how things aren't always as they seem to be. These two "friends" did not really get along well together and I was a pawn between the two of them being used as an added source of income and an extra pair of hands. Ultimately it became too much for me and I began to look for another job. Soon thereafter these two "friends" split up and went separate ways. In Denver the two partners played 'Mutt and Jeff' when it was actually 'Mutt hates Jeff and they both enjoy using Ron.'

I had interviewed in Rapid City, South Dakota when I first finished training in Jackson, Mississippi. I rejected it because it seemed to be a strange situation with a madman in charge. I should have listened to myself. I didn't. I wanted out of an ugly situation in Denver and the madman had alienated his former partner who had left and thus he needed help in his practice. There was plenty of work to do. What I did not realize was that I would be doing it all.

I found the best CD shop in the world there and visited it regularly. Yet as one of my patients, Arlin, was fond of saying, before she died at a young age from her disease, it was "a campground for f____d-up rejects."

Being that it was such a place, it seemed to have attracted people who had that meanness in their very core. One of those was My Sweet Gaelic Breeze's Obstetrician. I suppose I should thank him. Because of his mean-ness and unkindness a newborn was newly born in Cleveland, Ohio where we were able to rejoin an old Ob-Gyn and his loving care.

Going to Rapid City was a mistake which followed me around for quite some time. Even later after the diagnosis of Multiple Sclerosis had both My Sweet Gaelic Breeze and myself running back to be closer to the only parent we had left who acted like a parent—my father—it was still there lurking. When I returned to Spokane I was still capable and needed to work. We organized a Surgical Office. I planned to do General and Noncardiac Thoracic (Chest) Surgery. In that way I would not expose myself (or my patients) to the vicissitudes of my doing substandard—in my view—heart surgery. The stress made my illness worse and I realized it even then.

Trying to get hospital privileges while Phail T. Crecere was in and out of psychiatric hospitals in Northern California was quite the chore. He and his wife divorced, then he and the new partner in similar fashion split the sheets. The new partner, as he left encouraged the nurse and office help to go with him. I must say that that was good for them.

Robin K. Dhillon, M.D., M.B.A.

Nugent Came Back

Many years ago Ted Nugent did a rock concert in Spokane, Washington. During the concert an audience member who had come in with a gun, shot 'the Nuge.' After this Ted Nugent was quoted as saying the one place he wanted to go back to was Spokane, the place he got shot. They both believed in guns.

In many ways, as I reflect upon it now, I believe I was crazier than the Nuge. I ran to a community already overflowing with physicians and surgeons, with a transient community and a diminishing farming community, and a miniscule and declining health insurance base and thought I could practice as a surgeon with the mentality of the 1950s. Back then a surgeon needed the four 'As' which were: Availability, Affability, Affordability, and Ability. I was available twenty-four hours a day, seven days a week. I had always been affable. I loved people and helping them get better was my avocation—my calling. I was certainly affordable. Most of the time I worked for free as it turned out and I would suppose that that is more than affordable. I had often demonstrated, for the world and for myself, my ability during the long years of training.

We moved to Spokane to be close to the only family we thought we had left after the shock of a new diagnosis of Multiple Sclerosis and its unknown portents for the future. I was still walking and talking and had the full use of my fingers and my faculties. I began a solo surgical practice in a town inundated with physicians. In retrospect I believe I was unfair to them by intruding into their world. Still it was something I had to do and, thankfully, my soul mate and wife supported me in doing it. Ultimately, I would decide, when I developed numbness in all ten of my fingers, that I should no longer do surgery as it was not safe or fair for patients and, as a poster quoting Ken Griffey, Jr. (who also moved from Washington to Ohio for all the right reasons and counter to the flow of the almighty dollar) I once saw said, "doing what is right is never wrong."

Michael, John, Wayne, and Me

After years of training and practice in cardiothoracic surgery I had learned to view the operating field through my loupes. Loupes are, essentially, magnifying glasses, which magnify the operating field. At the same time that they magnify the operating field, allowing surgeons to see very small structures and to operate on them (as in doing fine surgical procedures on coronary blood vessels and pulmonary (lung) structures), it also restricts the surgeons' field of view. In other words, all one can see is that restricted field of view. The big picture is something one can only see by looking over one's loupes and the better surgeons who have to wear loupes for their work can only sense what is going on around them with their other senses, excluding vision. All that occurs has to be appreciated with one's senses of hearing, touch, smell, and taste because one's vision is occupied by the task at hand—operating. To see the big picture one has to look over one's loupes and in doing so one ends up having to refocus one's vision to a longer focal length and then to return to doing surgery on fine structures the process has to be done again in reverse, looking back through one's loupes. This can be extremely wasteful of time and also quite dangerous to the fine nature of the surgeon's work. As a result, to do the finest quality of work, i.e., the quality of work that every patient deserves, it is best to not look anywhere else but through one's loupes. One day, I looked over my loupes. What I saw was the loves of my life—my wife and children—and I realized that life like a waterfall was cascading away out of my view and gaining speed as it got farther away from me. My choice at that juncture was either to refocus through my loupes or back on surgery or to follow this waterfall that is life with my wife and children. I preferred the waterfall.

Not too long after I looked over my loupes my disease gave me a wonderful gift. Because of my disease I lost the fine sensation in my fingertips. At first it was not an insurmountable problem because it only affected my left thumb and forefinger. All my other fingers were just as sensitive as they had been before and supplied me with a great deal of information, allowing me to perform delicate surgery. I was able to continue to do high quality surgery—a standard to which I always held myself. Then, my disease, took away the sensation in all ten of my fingers. With that I could no longer do surgery safely for my patients. So I decided that the best thing to do was to stop doing surgery. I realized then that it would most likely be the most difficult thing I had ever done. That it was. Still, the end result is, after a journey through darkness, like a train in a tunnel, that I find that there is light at the end of the tunnel (and it is not an oncoming train). The light for me illuminates each day by shining on the beauty and activities of my wife, my daughter, and my two sons. And that is only the beginning. There are also many neighbors, their children, fam-

Robin K. Dhillon, M.D., M.B.A.

ily, their children, friends, and their children, and so many more wonderful beings just waiting to be discovered.

I thought to myself one day in 1999, "Hmmmm, Michael Jordan retired, John Elway retired, Wayne Gretsky retired, hmmmm," then why not me! Of course, they retired with millions of dollars and smiles on their faces. At least I had the smile (or at least a hope of getting one back). That has been my joke ever since. Nineteen-ninety-nine was a big year for Michael Jordan, John Elway, Wayne Gretsky, and.... me. We all wowed our field and then retired early. The day they announced their retirement they cried. I cried also. For almost nine months I cried in some fashion or another. In doing so I lost a little over fifty pounds, spent most of my days depressed, and sorely missed my glory days of doing surgery. I harkened back to the first cardiac surgical case I did in 1992. I was still a thoracic surgical resident at the time but the cardiac surgery resident was away and I was covering for him. The patient was an adult with an atrial septal defect. This is a relatively simple defect to repair and my attending surgeon on this case was the chief of cardiothoracic surgery and an expert at congenital heart surgery he was extremely well versed in repairing these defects in babies. He assisted and I did the case. At the end I remember him looking up and announcing to the room, "One minute he could not pronounce cardiac surgeon, and now he are one." Even laughing at myself it felt good and I felt proud of what I had done. This is something I learned during my years of depending on myself. I loved learning, participating in life, and contributing to my loved ones and all those around me; to paraphrase myself, "If you cannot laugh at yourself, you cannot laugh."

Before The End of These Days

As I have evolved I have noticed not only my surroundings but also a great many things about the multitude of lives around me. This has been truly fascinating to watch and to learn about all of these lives. At first the lives I appreciated most were immediately around me—my wife and children—and then, slowly, but surely I recognize many other lives, all with interesting, and in many ways, educational stories. Everyone from the new babies brought home by the neighbors to the new neighbors. Often times it would simply be the baby sitting two pews ahead of me in church who would carry on oblivious to the surroundings with an intense interest in their own fourth toe on their left foot after their feet escaped from their shoes. Learning about each of my own children has been a new challenge leading me into the future and providing a fascinating new experience. This has been another lesson that has been, partly a gift from my illness and the change in life it wrought. A gift of sight. Almost like sight for the blind. If not physically blind, spiritually blind.

I decided one day, after having met Father O., who is the first priest I ever felt I could believe and trust, that I would pursue my own discovery of God through Catholicism. First I would speak to him about my intellectual travails and journey so far. He would become the first human being besides my soul mate, my friend, my wife, with whom I would discuss my religious beliefs and difficulties. This, most likely, goes against the grain for many people in many ways but it raised many interesting thoughts for me. My parents never spent the time with me to provide me with any religious instruction. They did not include Judaism because they had no exposure to it. I have since had a great deal of exposure to all religions of the world, including Judaism. From what I have seen and after a great deal of thought I have concluded that there are no easy answers and that, truly, faith is simply a matter of faith and nothing more. Nobody can create a scientific proof of matters of faith and, in fact, this would run counter to the essence of faith. Faith requires no proof. It requires faith.

Like a pebble thrown into a stream the ripples expand outward incessantly and effervescently. After I had spoken to Father O. and had decided to follow my path of religious discovery I decided to tell my daughter of my change of thought and belief. The smile on her face was beauteous and had long been absent from our home. It made me happy again. Little did I know that later she would confide that after such a troublesome year as we had all had this was to be a very special moment for her and made her as happy as she could ever remember being. Once again, it seems, what is right is right and it requires no proof a priori.

Robin K. Dhillon, M.D., M.B.A.

While learning about each of the children I also learned about myself. As intensely as My Sweet Gaelic Breeze and I prepare for each day in our children's lives and for each transition they make as they grow I realize what it means to swim in the ocean surrounded by water with nary a drop to drink. I grew up with two loving parents who had extremely busy lives where their main foci were themselves and their lives. Certainly it was a feature of the time in their lives and what they needed to do to support their family and their lives. I suppose, in many ways, I was advanced beyond my time and needed what parents like My Sweet Gaelic Breeze and myself have to offer in the 21st century. In a manner of speaking, I grew up surrounded by a loving family in the midst of an orphanage.

There are a great many things I hope to see and do before the end of these days. Somehow I have had the great fortune to have a vision of life thrust upon me that comes to many at the end of life but to only a few this early in life. I am amazed at the multitudes of people that seem to expand in numbers each day, the paucity of understanding of the wonder of life, and the number of people on both sides of the coin—knowing and unknowing—who do not realize or recognize that life exists right in front of them—a spouse to love, children to nurture, people all around to teach and learn from—and all around them. Life is not better with two dollars instead of one. It is not a hedonistic adventure where you, the protagonist, have everything and get everything that 'everyone' wants. 'Everyone' turns out to be one person without any sense of modesty or respect for the multitude of other people who also breathe 'our' air. Today's movies reflect a nonsensical, imaginary life of nonsensical, imaginary people. In Ireland, the pubs are family gathering places where the family goes, Mama, Papa, and all the children to read the paper, talk, play, and laugh with other Mamas, Papas, and children and, maybe, have a pint or two (Mama and Papa, at least, for this last activity). In the fast-paced world of America, men go to bars to drink, watch sports, and meet women who aren't their wives, women go to drink, to get away from their children, and to meet men who aren't as dull as their husbands, and if children go, they end up meeting with social services. Life like a car ride takes a lot of turns, sometimes goes too fast, and sometimes goes too slow. Lately my car ride seemed to be going down, down, down, but now it seems to be heading back up again. As I head back up I can see the many valleys and smaller mountains below. I realize that I have scaled them all, up and down, and now am, virtually, flying so I can alight wherever I wish and enjoy the beauties and pleasures of all that there is to enjoy on the wide panorama of earth. I have the steering wheel and the gearshift in my hands and my feet alternating between the clutch, the brake pedal, and the accelerator. It is up to me to travel any road I wish to travel. I can turn right, left, or continue on straight ahead (or, as one of my best friends growing up always used to say, "Forward, never straight." The response that I came up with, almost thirty years later—a little tongue in cheek—is "Yeah, I'll drink to that!" Thinking that I would laugh as I raise a pint with my wife and the children reflected in my glass.). Interestingly, on the news recently one of the most common and desirable areas for people to move to and rated as one of the best new family areas to live is Ireland.

One day in the year 2000 I woke up. This awakening was not just opening my eyes in the morning but more so an arousal from a year of rest and hibernation. Today I know that my mind and my body needed this rest very badly. Along with the blessings of my disease, I have discovered numerous other blessings as well. Last night I saw the stars in the night sky again for the first time in what seems like an eternity. They are beautiful. On our deck there are flowers—Purple Passion Petunias—which I selected. Today I can appreciate their beauty. Yesterday, I could not.

I have never been a 'car guy,' but, recently, I bought a car. A car that in my yesterdays I would have never bought. I must confess, my wife made me do it. I may have voiced her praise before but I am singing loud and proud now. It is a sporty little convertible and I even named it. I love my car. It makes me smile and for the first time in my life I do not even have to go fast. The speed limit, even if it is too slow for the rest of the workaday world, is just fine with me. I will get there when I get there. I will get there whole with myself, my car, and everybody else in one piece. The only hullabaloo will be the sounds coming out of the in-dash stereo and the only wildness will be in my head bobbing to the music.

Part of my awakening was a realization that I love not only my family but I also love me. In life there are still a few things that I would like to do that fall into a category of 'stuff I would like to do.'

I even want to work again. However, today I want to work at doing something I love to do. As a good friend said to me recently, "if your work is doing something you love to do, then you won't work a day of your life." That is quote, unquote from Ann Lande, whose second life was to become a surgeon, having been an engineer, and was in the process of beginning her third life. She was soon to enjoy being a mama to her little love child, Van, who had just turned two years old. We had been fellow surgical residents-in-training and seemed to always have some degree of this same relationship, being envious of each other's life's attributes. Somehow each one of us managed to always go where the other one wanted to or had been and was able to pass along tidbits of useful and useless knowledge. Both of us have never been certain, which was better, the useful or the useless knowledge.

Robin K. Dhillon, M.D., M.B.A.

For a brief period I was looking forward to working in a fellowship program, training in quality assessment in Medicine. In the course of applying for the program, despite having been given the job officially, I was subsequently officially and officiously "disapproved" for the position for rather mysterious reasons, which the powers that be would not elaborate. I suspect that the reasons were based on hearsay and unsubstantiated slander preventing those making the decision from presenting them and defending them. Regardless of their true nature, once again it seemed to be a sign from on high that this was not the path for me to follow. So I would begin to look elsewhere.

Regardless of where this search might lead I have found some profound truths and beauties along the way. Most recently I have been able to reflect on some metaphors which simply sprang into my thoughts, out of the blue, as it were, making me suspect that their source, or, at least, their inspiration, was Divine. This only comes to mind for me because it is so new to my existence and not for any special status that I have been accorded. No, if anything I have been allowed to join the mass of everyday humanity—truly a gift when you have lived your life amidst that mass of humanity without being a part of it. One of those metaphors came to me while talking to my sister-in-law over breakfast at one of the last 'real' diners anywhere. We were talking about life, specifically about our college experiences. I went to a four-year state university and in freshman year went to <u>every</u> class. I never sat in the first row—always in the back where I could read something else, nap, and leave. By the time I reached my senior year I barely went to class at all. I spent more time shooting pool, playing pinball machines and foosball, smoking cigarettes, and drinking coffee. To me it was like surfing. You have to swim out and get to the top of the big wave so you can ride it as far as you can before crashing into the beach and having to start over again. Of course, the great surfers—visionaries of the beach—saw the big waves coming and positioned themselves so they could catch them as they were just building up speed and size. Every step of the way—with each stroke out to the top of a wave—I have felt the elation of getting to the top of the wave and the thrill of riding it out. Sometimes it has been difficult to truly spot the end of the ride, but God in his wisdom placed the beach as a, sometimes, harsh end to the ride; but always a comfortable and comforting location to hang out while enjoying the trail you have just traveled. It is always a matter of time and perspective.

With that time and perspective I realize I have a lot to be thankful for and to praise. Most of all I walked the walk and I talked the talk once. And I have come to realize that few among us cannot say that in some fashion and in some context. Even though I do not do it now, I did it then and though my life has changed, as have I, it is still a wondrous thing.

(Endnotes)
1. http://www.cuti.com.my/Sub/Pahang/ph_map.htm
2. http://en.wikipedia.org/wiki/Pahang
3. http://www.allaboutguadalajara.com/
4. this is an often repeated saying in many Surgical Rounds and Morbidity & Mortality Meetings (in Academic Surgical Centers these are usually conducted weekly with the intent to review any mistakes or unusual occurrences so that these can be avoided or prevented by others).
5. http://vive.guadalajara.gob.mx/historia/indexi.html
6. From the Old Irish sentiment that Grandma Annette always quoted that when God closes one door He always opens another

A Life … And An …

After Life

www.ingramcontent.com/pod-product-compliance
Lightning Source LLC
Chambersburg PA
CBHW081349040426
42450CB00015B/3366